Science in Ancient India

Melissa Stewart

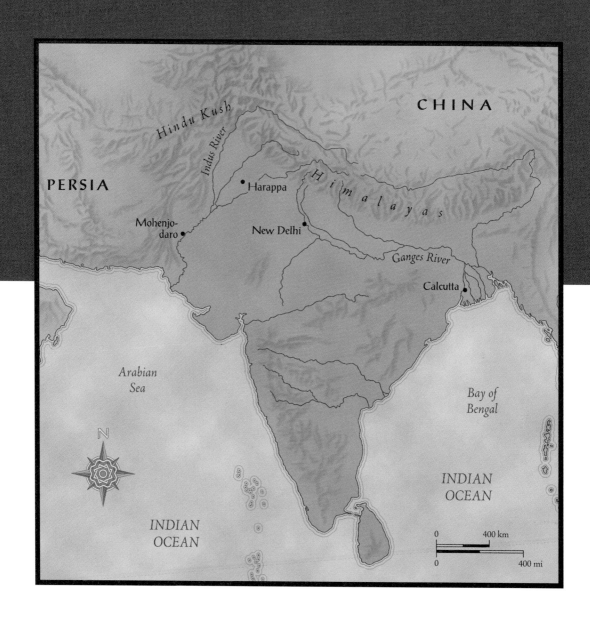

Science in Ancient India

Melissa Stewart

Science of the Past

FRANKLIN WATTS
A Division of Grolier Publishing
New York • London • Hong Kong • Sydney
Danbury, Connecticut

Visit Franklin Watts on the Internet at: http://publishing.grolier.com

Photographs ©: Ancient Art & Architecture Collection Ltd.: 30 (Richard Sheridan), 31; Art Resource: 8, 9, 13 (Borromeo), 10 (Erich Lessing), cover (Scala), 12 (Victoria & Albert Museum), 56 (Werner Forman Archive), 38; Children's Press: 26; Corbis-Bettmann: 19, 34; Dinodia Picture Agency: 6 (Sunil S. Kapadia), 11, 18, 23, 27, 35 (Milind A. Ketkar), 20; e.t. archive: 15, 55; North Wind Picture Archives: 14, 43; Photo Researchers: 28 (Biophoto Associates/Science Source), 42 (Jerry Schad) 48 (Chris Bjornberg), 41 (George Past/SPL), 22 (Perlstein/Jerrican), 24 (SPL); Stock Montage, Inc.: 51; Superstock, Inc.: 47, 50; Tony Stone Images: 36 (Doug Armand), 37 (Warren Bolster), 52 (David Hanson), 46 (A & L Sinibaldi), UPI/Corbis-Bettmann: 39.

Map created by XNR Productions Inc.

Library of Congress Cataloging-in-Publication Data

Stewart, Melissa
Science in ancient India / Melissa Stewart.
p. cm.—(Science of the past)
Includes bibliographical references and index.
Summary: An overview of the scientific contributions of ancient India including Arabic numerals, ayurveda, basic chemistry and physics, and celestial observations.
ISBN 0-531-11626-3
1. Science ancient—Juvenile literature. 2. Science—India—Juvenile literature. 3. India—Civilization—Juvenile literature. [1. Science, Ancient. 2. Science—India—History. 3. India—Civilization.] I. Title. II. Series.
Q124.95.S75   1999
509.34—dc21   98-18536
                                                                  CIP
                                                                  AC

CONTENTS

chapter 1
India Through the Ages

The Indus River was the center of
the Indus Valley civilization.

India is one of the most unique places in the world. In some ways, India is as much a culture and a spirit as a specific land area. Historically, India was bordered by the Himalaya and Hindu Kush mountains in the north, the Arabian Sea on the west, the Bay of Bengal on the east, and the Indian Ocean on south. As a result, India was sort of like an island—completely separate from the rest of Asia. That is why many people still refer to India as a "subcontinent."

It was not until the 1900s that the mountainous regions north of modern-day India became separate nations. In fact, the name "India" comes from the Indus River, which flows through what is now Pakistan.

The Indus Valley Civilization

The *civilization* that began to develop along the Indus River about 6,000 years ago is the oldest in India, and among the oldest in the world. As the ancient Indians improved their farming methods, the Indus Valley civilization grew and spread in all directions. By 4,500 years ago, it was the largest civilization in the world and had two capital cities.

Harappa and Mohenjo-daro were well-planned cities with large streets that ran from north to south or east to west. People lived in brick houses that were two or three stories tall. Inside each home was an open courtyard surrounded by several rooms. A city-wide sewer system ran beneath the main streets, and every home had indoor toilets and baths.

Each city had a central area protected by strong brick walls. Inside the walls were granaries that held crops from the last harvest, religious buildings with impressive altars, and a variety of government buildings. Most of

the food eaten by the people living in these communities was grown in the fertile land along the Indus River. The major crops were wheat, barley, dates, and melons.

A surplus of food made it possible for some of the people to devote all their time to other jobs. Merchants sold some goods to local people and prepared the rest for export to the Middle East. Breadmakers spent their days baking, while metalworkers and potters made coins, religious statues, jewelry, and toys. *Archaeologists* have found examples of all these objects as well as dozens of sandstone seals with carvings of animals and symbols.

No one knows exactly how the earliest Indians, dark-skinned people called Dravidians, used these seals.

The Indus Valley civilization flourished for about 1,000 years, and then mysteriously disappeared. Harappa seems to have been destroyed suddenly. It may have fallen victim to a flood, an earthquake, or an attack by invaders. Mohenjo-daro appears to have declined more slowly. There is evidence that in its last years, the buildings were often sloppily patched together. The city may have been abandoned because surrounding farmland was no longer fertile or because it was slowly overrun by invaders.

Like their ancient ancestors the Aryans, some modern Indians spend their days herding sheep and cattle.

The Aryans Move into India

Who could these invaders have been? Around 3,500 years ago, a group of light-skinned people called Aryans came to India through passages in the Hindu Kush mountains. Unlike the Dravidians, the Aryans were wandering herders. Over the next 500 years, the Aryans slowly moved southward until they reached the Ganges Valley in central India. As the Aryans invaded, they pushed the Dravidians farther and farther south. Eventually, the Aryans began to settle down and farm.

Although the Aryans seemed to have no written language, they developed a large body of sacred poems and hymns called the *Vedas*. The *Vedas* record how the Aryans reacted to, and interacted with, the world around them. These poems also describe the Indo-Aryan way of life, including how people were divided into social groups called *castes*, based on the kind of work they did. The *Vedas* even discuss ideas about the origin of the universe and recommend herbal remedies for some common illnesses.

Most importantly, the *Vedas* contain the basic ideas that underlie a religion called Hinduism. For many modern Indians, Hinduism is more than a religion—it is a way of life. India has long been a land that accepts, and even welcomes, diversity. Today, there are fourteen official languages, at least three major religons, and traditions that find their origins in more than a dozen different cultures. In a nation with so many cultural differences, the Hindu lifestyle remains an important unifying force.

These books explain the ancient Indian *Vedas*.

Brahma, the all-seeing god

Hinduism, which has its roots in the *Vedas*, developed slowly over a 1,000-year period. Modern Hinduism was influenced by a number of cultures and religions. Although the religion recognizes more than 1,000 gods and goddesses, most Hindus worship only a few of them. The most essential traditional gods are Brahma, Vishnu, and Shiva.

Hindus believe that a soul never dies. When a body dies, the soul is reborn until it reaches spiritual perfection, which is called *nirvana*. The process of being reborn is called *reincarnation.* Hindus believe that a human being can be reincarnated as any other animal—a pig, a chicken, a frog, a fish, or even an insect. For this reason, most Hindus do not eat meat. Hindus also believe that everything a person does has a consequence—in this life and in later lives. Good deeds are rewarded and bad deeds are punished. This idea is called *karma.*

Between the years 300 and 600, Dravidian kings in southern India came to value the opinions of Hindu priests and scholars. As a result, most Indians eventually adopted ideas that had Aryan origins. Thus, modern Hinduism is a blend of ancient Aryan and Dravidian ways of thinking.

Hinduism was also influenced by the ideas of Gautama Siddharta Buddha, who lived about 2,500 years ago. Buddha's ideas eventually evolved into Buddhism—a separate religion that spread to the Far East and is still very popular in that part of the world. In India, however, Buddhist ideas were absorbed by Hinduism. Buddha believed that everyone should strive to be loving, compassionate, and tolerant of all other people. The Hindu ideas of reincarnation, nirvana, and karma were probably borrowed from Buddhism. Similarly, the Hindu idea that all living things have a soul may have been borrowed from Jainism, an Indian religon that developed around the same time as Buddhism.

This statue of Buddha is on display at the National Museum in New Delhi, India.

Alexander the Great meeting Porus, the Persian ruler of India

While Hinduism was developing in central India, a new group of invaders began to conquer northern India. About 2,500 years ago, King Darius I of Persia entered northwestern India. For the next 200 years, the northernmost regions of India were invaded by many different groups of people. About 2,300 years ago, Alexander the Great, the ruler of the Greek Empire,

The symbol of the Mauryan leader Ashoka was three lions, each looking out over a different part of the empire.

conquered a large region of northern India. When Alexander died just 3 years later, the Indians realized that they finally had a chance to unite and rule themselves. Chandragupta Maurya was the man who made this vision a reality. Eventually, the Mauryan Empire included most of India.

The Great Empires

The greatest Mauryan ruler was Ashoka, the grandson of Chandragupta. Horrified by the terrors of war, Ashoka converted to Buddhism and traveled widely, listening to the ideas and concerns of his people. During his reign, India built the first free hospitals and veterinary clinics. Ashoka also planted thousands of trees for shade and to control *erosion*. After

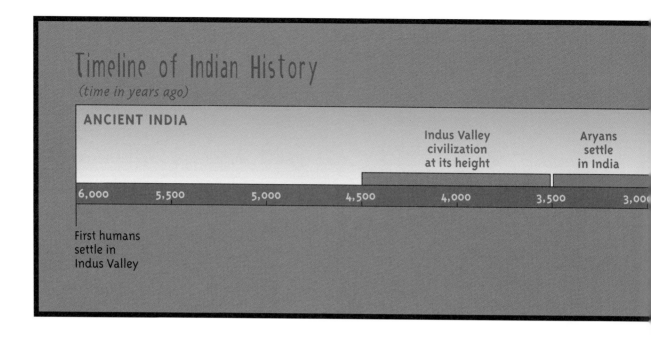

Timeline of Indian History
(time in years ago)

ANCIENT INDIA

Indus Valley civilization at its height

Aryans settle in India

6,000   5,500   5,000   4,500   4,000   3,500   3,00

First humans settle in Indus Valley

Ashoka's death, the empire began to weaken. About 100 years later, the last Mauryan ruler was assassinated by an army commander.

Over the next 500 years, India was split into many small kingdoms, each with its own ruler. Finally, around the year 320 another great empire began to develop. Like the Mauryan Empire, the Gupta Empire eventually included most of India. The Gupta Empire is generally considered the golden age of Indian history. During this period, India was possibly the happiest and most civilized place in the world. The first Indian universities were established and literature, art, architecture, and science flourished.

The greatest ruler of the Gupta Empire was Chandragupta II. He promoted peace and encouraged his people to create great works of art and study the world around them. Some of the greatest Indian mathematicians, *astronomers,* and doctors lived and worked during this era.

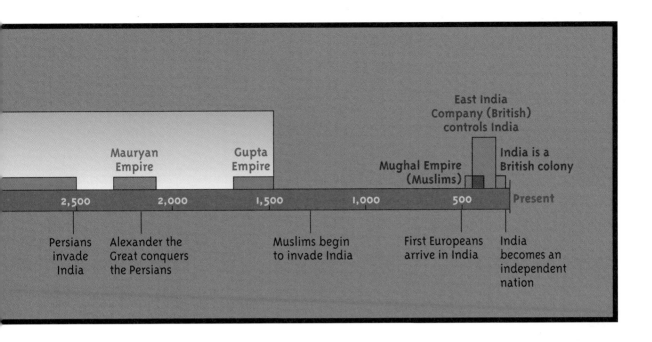

Eventually, foreign invaders and internal struggles began to weaken the Gupta Empire. Historians say that India's ancient period ended when the Gupta Empire fell in 540, but it is impossible to say that this was the end of the Indian civilization. Although *Muslims* from various parts of the Middle East, British traders, and finally the British government ran India's government for the next 1,400 years, these foreigners could never conquer the spirit that has long been described with just one word—India.

chapter 2
medicine in Ancient India

The *Vedas* contain the earliest information about an ancient Indian healing system called ayurveda. Ayurveda is still practiced today in India and some other parts of the world.

Medicine is generally considered the oldest Indian science. Its roots can be traced back more than 3,000 years. The *Vedas* mention many of the ideas included in a system of healing called *ayurveda,* which means "the science of long life."

What is Ayurveda?

According to ayurveda, the body consists of five natural elements—earth (bones and muscles), water (mucus), fire *(bile),* wind (breath), and space (hollow organs). Water, fire, and wind are the active elements. As long as they are in harmony, a person is healthy. A person gets sick when the balance between the active elements is disturbed.

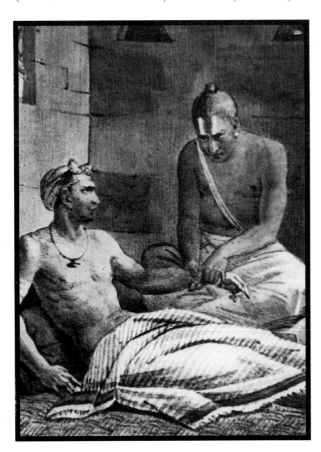

An ancient Indian healer treating a patient

Medical treatments consisted of remedies made from plants and other natural materials. Because they were designed to work with the body's natural mechanisms, the remedies worked gradually over a period of time and caused fewer side effects than most modern drugs. Ayurvedic healers tried to provide remedies that would help the body to heal itself.

Herbal medicines made from ingredients like the ones shown here worked with the body to help heal patients.

Indian healers gave their patients treatments that relieved symptoms and also treated the underlying cause of the illness. Although this seems like common sense to us, at that time it was a revolutionary idea. More than 1,000 years passed before other cultures began to look for the underlying cause of a disease.

Some ancient Indian remedies have been scientifically proven to work. For example, oil from the bark of chaulmugra trees is still the most effective treatment for *leprosy*. A plant called amalaki was used to improve overall health and prevent scurvy, which is caused by a shortage of vitamin C. Today, we know that amalaki is the best natural source of vitamin C. Garlic was said to prevent premature aging and prolong life. Modern scientists agree that garlic can improve stamina and overall health. The table on page 21 lists some other ingredients used by ancient Indian healers.

Herbal Remedies

INGREDIENT	SOURCE	USE
Arka	Liquor made from sugar, fruit, and roots	Anesthetize patients during surgery
Biscobra	Snake venom	Treat snakebites
Camphor	Wood and bark of camphor tree	Clean wounds, insect repellent
Googul	Gummy substance from plant	Hold many medications together
Honey long	From beehives	Flavor medications, promote life
Jatamansi	Root	Increase appetite
Kachnar	Bark of acacia tree	Relieve sore throat
Macir	Bark	Treat diarrhea
Spikenard	Oil from plant	Give pleasant scent to remedies, increase growth and blackness of hair
Tamarind	Fruit	Flavor many medicinal drinks
Vasak	Oil from plant	Relieve cough, improve breathing

Ancient Indians knew that the best way to live longer was to prevent illnesses, rather than just treat them when they occurred. That is why all Indians considered hygiene very important. They chewed on twigs from the neem tree to clean their teeth and strengthen their gums, and they were the first people to shampoo their hair. Ancient Indians bathed frequently, often once a day.

Yoga is still practiced today in many parts of the world.

A Look at Yoga

As Hinduism spread, more and more Indians began to practice yoga. Yoga, a strict program of eating and exercising, is believed to improve overall mental and physical health. The exercises involve a specific routine of breathing and holding the body in various positions for a period of time. They were designed to condition, tone, and strengthen the body as well as to reduce stress, promote relaxation, and create awareness.

Yoga can help people stay physically fit and strong enough to avoid many illnesses. Modern doctors agree that yoga increases general health and can prevent—or even cure—some diseases. No one knows how or when yoga began. The first written text describing the program is about 2,100 years old. The yoga tradition has been kept alive for centuries by devout Hindus, Buddhists, and Jainists. Today, people all over the world practice yoga.

Charaka's Contribution to Medicine

The first Indian medical text was written about 1,900 years ago by Charaka, the court physician of King Kanishka. According to legend, Charaka was famous for saving the king's wife. The doctor's book, now called *Charaka Samhita* meaning "Work of Charaka," contains medical knowledge acquired by healers over hundreds of years. Some of the information may have been passed down from healers who lived more than 2,800 years ago.

Charaka Samhita includes a complete explanation of ayurveda as well as instructions about how doctors should treat their patients. It says, "You must not betray your patient, even at the cost of your life. . . . Nothing that happens in the house of a patient can be recounted outside, nor may you report your patient's condition to anyone who might do him any harm by virtue of that knowledge."

These books contain the text of *Charaka Samhita* translated into Sanskrit, the most popular language in modern India.

These words are strikingly similar to those written by another great healer of the ancient world. Hippocrates, who lived about 2,500 years ago in Greece, also wrote that a doctor should respect and protect his patients' privacy. Today, all physicians must take an oath, called the Hippocratic oath, to treat their patients fairly.

After Alexander the Great invaded India, the exchange of spices, precious metals, and ideas between Greece and India was common. There is no way to determine whether Hippocrates' ideas influenced Charaka or whether these ideas were passed down to him from the earliest Indian healers.

Other sections of the *Charaka Samhita* discuss diarrhea, fever, swelling, tuberculosis,

The ancient Greek physician Hippocrates is sometimes referred to as the "father of Western medicine."

tumors, wound infection, *epilepsy*, leprosy, *jaundice,* and skin diseases. More general sections describe the body's structure and how it functions. The ancient Indians knew quite a bit about the skeletal system, but less about the organs. They believed that the heart, not the brain, was the center of thought and intelligence. Charaka's book shows a basic understanding of how the body digests food and of simple *genetics*— Charaka knew that physical features are passed from parents to their children.

Still other sections described how to treat mentally ill patients, analyze dreams, care for pregnant women, and nourish patients. Charaka also discussed how climate, diet, and other environmental factors can affect health. He said, "A physician . . . should first study all the factors, including environment, which influence a patient's disease, and then prescribe a treatment. It is more important to prevent the occurrence of disease than to seek a cure." Only after completing these steps should the doctor recommend a remedy.

Surgery in Ancient India

The first Indian work describing surgical practices was written by a physician named Sushruta. Because Charaka's work does not mention surgery at all, many historians believe that surgical techniques developed after his death. As a result, some historians claim that Sushruta lived during the Gupta Period. Other historians believe that Sushruta lived much earlier— possibly 2,700 years ago. They claim that Charaka's work does not mention surgery because he considered surgeons and ayurvedic doctors to have unrelated occupations.

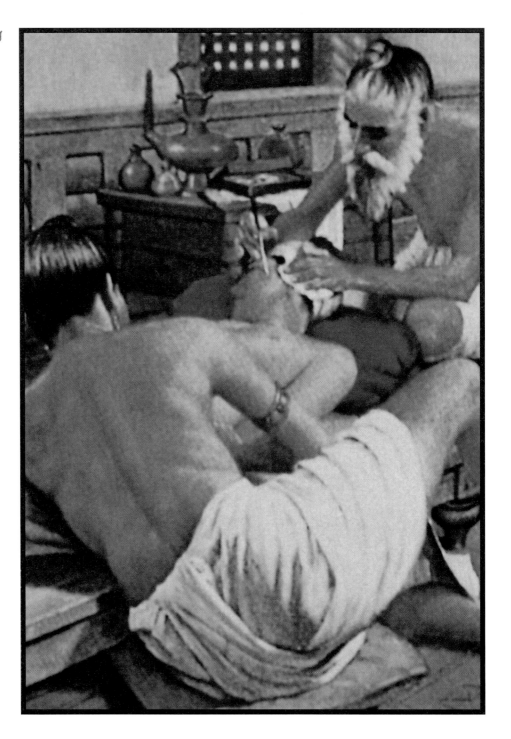

Sushruta treating a patient

26

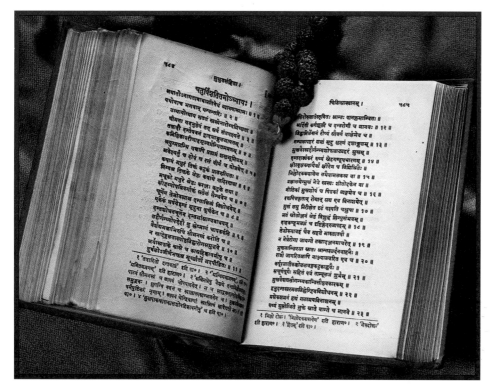

This Sanskrit translation of *Sushruta Samhita* explains Sushruta's method for removing cataracts and performing plastic surgery.

No matter when Sushruta lived, his manuscript, *Sushruta Samhita,* shows that surgical techniques were extremely advanced in ancient India. He mentions more than 125 surgical instruments and 14 types of bandages. To learn how the body's parts worked, Indian surgeons often dissected corpses. Sushruta's work explains how the body was prepared for study.

A perfectly preserved body must be used. It should be the body of a person who is not very old and did not die of poison or severe disease. After the intestines have been cleared, the body must be wrapped in tree bark, grass, or hemp and placed in a cage for protection against animals. The cage should be placed in a carefully concealed spot in a river with a fairly gentle current, and the body left to soften.

After 7 days, the body should be removed from the water. Using a brush made of grass roots, hair, and bamboo, the body should be brushed off a layer at a time. In this way, the eye can observe every part of the body— beginning with the skin—as each part is laid bare by brushing.

Sushruta's work also describes procedures for setting broken bones, amputating infected arms and legs, extracting infected teeth, draining and stitching large wounds, and removing *cataracts* of the eye. The following passage from Sushruta's book is a detailed description of an operation to remove a cataract of the eye:

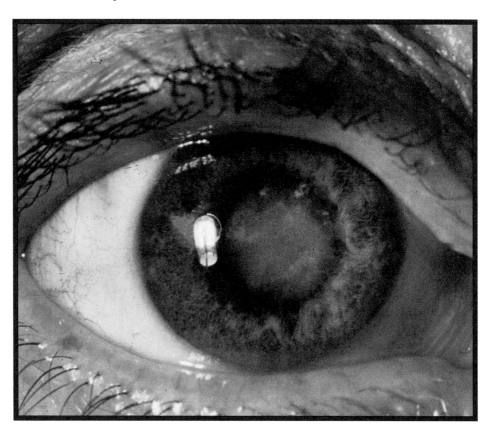

A patient with a cataract

It was a bright morning. The surgeon sat on a bench. The patient sat on the ground in front of the doctor, so that the doctor was at a comfortable height for doing the operation on the patient's eye. After eating and washing, the patient was tied so that he could not move during the operation.

The doctor breathed on the patient's eye to warm it up and then rubbed it with his thumb. He asked the patient to look straight ahead. While assistants held the patient's head firmly, the doctor chose a scalpel. The cataract was in the patient's left eye, so the doctor would use his right hand for the operation.

The doctor held the knife with his forefinger, middle finger, and thumb and inserted it into the patient's eye. The scalpel entered exactly where it should—half a finger's length from the black of the eye and a quarter of a finger's length from the outer corner of the eye. The doctor moved the scalpel gracefully—first back and forth, then up. There was a small sound and a drop of liquid came out.

The doctor spoke a few words to comfort the patient and moistened the eye with milk. The doctor scratched the pupil with the tip of the scalpel. This motion did not hurt the patient. The doctor pushed the slimy cataract material out of the patient's eye.

It was a matter of joy for the patient that he could see objects through his operated eye. The doctor drew the scalpel out of the patient's eye slowly. He then laid cotton soaked in fat on the wound and placed a bandage over it.

Sushruta was best known for his ability to reconnect ears and noses that had been cut off as a form of punishment. The procedures in Sushruta's text are the earliest descriptions of plastic surgery. In fact, Sushruta's attached-flap method is still used to reattach fingers, limbs, ears, and noses today.

Muslims recognized the benefits of the Indian system of numbers and began using it. Later, they introduced the system to Europeans.

Arabic Numerals Come from India

The world owes a huge debt to ancient Indian mathematicians. The system of counting numbers we use today was developed in ancient India about 2,200 years ago. During the Gupta Empire, this system was refined to include a symbol for nothing—zero—and the idea of *place value*.

When Muslims from the Middle East invaded India after the Gupta Empire fell, they realized that the Indian counting system was superior to their own. The Muslims adopted the Indian system and introduced it to Spaniards about 1,100 years ago. The rest of western Europe learned about this counting system about 200 years later. Because the Middle East was once known as Arabia, we call the symbols used in this number system *Arabic numerals.*

Before learning about Arabic numerals, people in western Europe used many different numerical systems. The Greeks, who had influenced people in the area surrounding the Mediterranean Sea, used letters of their alphabet to stand for numbers. The Romans, who had conquered most of Europe as well as parts of Africa and Asia, also used a system based on letters.

This mosque was built in Córdoba, Spain, after the city was conquered by the Muslims.

Numeric Symbols

ARABIC	GREEK	ROMAN
1	A	I
2	B	II
3	Γ	III
4	Δ	IV
5	E	V
6	F	VI
7	Z	VII
8	H	VIII
9	Θ	IX
10	I	X
20	K	XX
30	Λ	XXX
40	M	XL
50	N	L
60	Ξ	LX
70	O	LXX
80	Π	LXXX
90	Q	XC
100	P	C

The system of counting numbers developed in ancient India was much simpler than those used by the ancient Greeks and Romans. The Indian system used just nine different number symbols plus the zero. As a result, it was possible to write any number—no matter how large or small it might be.

Like many other number systems, the Indian method of counting was based on the number ten, probably because people have ten fingers. What makes the Indian system so special is that the value of a numeral is determined by its position, or place, within a number. This idea is called place value.

For example, when the symbol 4 appears alone, it always means four units. But when it is followed by another number symbol, such as 6, the four represents tens. We read the number as 46 (forty-six). And when the symbol 4 is followed by two number symbols, such as 6 and 9, the four represents hundreds. In the number 469 (four hundred sixty-nine), the 4 symbol stands for hundreds, the 6 symbol stands for tens, and the 9 symbol stands for units.

According to this system, moving a number to the left increases its value by ten times. Thus, 40 is ten times greater than 4, 400 is ten times greater than 40, and 4,000 is ten times greater than 400.

This system would not work if the zero symbol did not exist. To us zero is just a number, but to the ancient Indians it was a brilliant solution to a difficult problem. It allowed them to write large numbers with just a few symbols.

The ancient Greeks, Romans, and Egyptians had no zero in their counting systems. As a result, it was very difficult for them to add, subtract, multiply, and divide large numbers. When we add 428 to 734, we add the numbers one column at a time—first 8 + 4, then 2 + 3, and finally 4 + 7—to arrive at a solution of 1,162. Other ancient numerical symbols could not be broken down into smaller values that were easier to handle.

How Higher Math Developed

The Muslims brought more than just Arabic numerals to the rest of the world. In his writings, a Muslim mathematician named Al-Khwarizmi explained the principles of a form of math he called "al-jabr." Today, we call this type of math *algebra* and most students learn about it in high school.

Like counting numbers, algebra was developed by ancient Indian mathematicians. In fact, the first mention of algebra is in the *Vedas,* where it is called "bijaganitam," which means "the other math" or "the second math." It is called the second math because it was developed after basic mathematics as a shorthand method for calculating the *area* of a rectangle, a circle, or a triangle. These shapes were often incorporated into altars built by Indo-Aryans when Hinduism was still a very young religion.

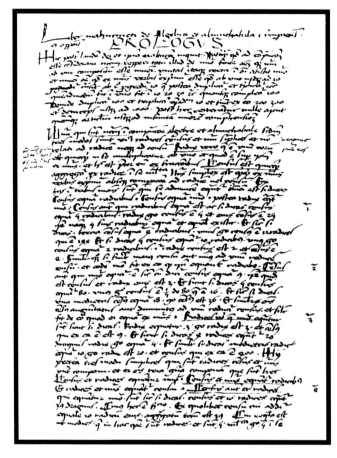

The first page of Al-Khwarizmi's book about algebra

Arybhata and Brahmagupta

Two of the most important Indian mathematicians are associated with the Gupta Period. Arybhata, who was born in 476, is best remembered for writing *Arybhatiya,* a summary of everything that Indian mathematicians had learned up to that time. It included information about the Indian counting system, basic arithmetic, and fractions. The book also described how to calculate the area of a triangle or a rectangle, the *volume* (amount of space

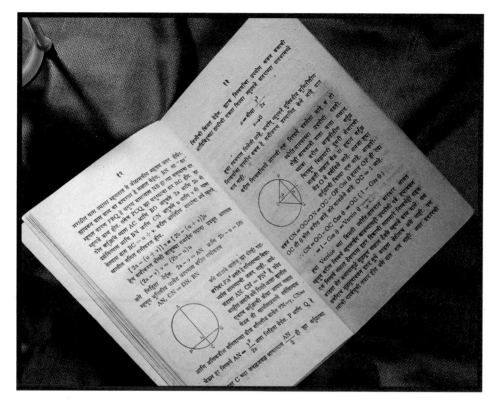

This version of *Arybhatiya* helps us understand what ancient Indians knew about mathematics.

inside) of a sphere—an object shaped like a ball, and the *circumference* (distance around the outside border) of a circle.

Although Brahmagupta was born in 598, after the Gupta Period was officially over, he is still considered part of India's golden age. Like Arybhata, he wrote about mathematics. His texts, which expand on some of Arybhata's ideas, show that he had a far better understanding of numbers and mathematics than anyone else of his time.

Brahmagupta was interested in more than just mathematics. As you will learn in the next chapter, he applied his knowledge of numbers to studying the stars. He was director of the astronomical observatory at Ujjain, the center of mathematics and space science in ancient India.

chapter 4
Applying Math to the Universe

Ancient Indian scientists knew a great deal about the stars and the solar system.

Using mathematics as a tool for studying the star-filled night sky did not originate with Brahmagupta. In the days of the *Vedas,* it seems that algebra was used to position religious altars with respect to certain stars.

The Order of the Universe

The *Vedas* and other ancient Indian texts show that early Indians understood that the only difference between the sun that they saw during the day and the stars they saw at night was their distance from Earth. According to one text, "When one sun sinks below the horizon, a thousand suns take its place."

The Ancient Indians understood that the sun we see during the day is the same as the stars that fill the night sky.

This painting of Ptolemy, an ancient Greek astronomer, was done by an Italian artist around 1475.

The ancient Indians also knew that the sun is at the center of our solar system. The *Vedas* refer to the sun as "the Master," "the source of all life," "the center of creation," and "the center of the spheres." (The "spheres" are probably the other planets.) Although some ancient Greeks also believed that the sun was at the center of our solar system, their ideas were overshadowed by those of Claudius Ptolaemeus, also known as Ptolemy. Ptolemy lived in Greece about 1,800 years ago. He claimed that Earth was at the center of the universe and that all the planets, the sun, and moon moved around Earth in perfect circles.

Because he was so well respected, Ptolemy convinced other Greek astronomers that his view

An artist's interpretation of how Ptolemy pictured the universe

of the universe was correct. Even though his charts were often wrong, it took more than 1,400 years to prove that the sun—not Earth—is at the center of our solar system. Thus, Indian astronomers were thousands of years ahead of the Europeans.

You see a full moon when the side that reflects sunlight is facing Earth.

Movement of Earth and the Moon

This is not all that the Indians knew about the universe. The *Arybhatiya*, which was completed around 499, describes Earth as a sphere that is constantly spinning. The author explains that the stars' apparent movement across the night sky is actually the result of Earth's own movement.

Arybhata also understood that moonlight is not generated by the moon. It is actually reflected light from the sun. The side of the moon that faces the sun is always bright, and the side that faces away from the sun is always dark. When the bright side of the moon faces the night side of Earth, you see a bright, glowing full moon. As the moon moves around Earth, you see less and less of the bright side. About 2 weeks after you see a full moon, you see only a sliver of moon. Then, one night, you see no moon at all.

When you see a "new moon," the bright side is turned completely away from Earth. Over the next couple of weeks, the moon appears to grow fuller and fuller each night. As the moon continues to circle Earth, more and more of its bright side is visible. The planets seem to glow and go through phases for the same reason.

This knowledge led Arybhata to understand what causes eclipses. A *solar eclipse*—an eclipse of the sun—occurs when the moon moves between Earth and the sun. When this happens during daylight hours, people can't help but notice. As the moon moves in front of the sun, the sun takes on the shape of a crescent. Before long, the sun disappears completely. A few minutes later, the sun reappears.

As the moon moves in front of the sun, the sun appears in the shape of a crescent that quickly shrinks away and then reappears.

During a lunar eclipse, the sun, Earth, and moon line up in such a way that the moon appears dark to viewers on Earth.

A *lunar eclipse*—an eclipse of the moon—occurs when Earth casts a shadow on the moon as it moves between the sun and the moon. The eclipse is visible from the side of Earth facing the moon—the night side. This is why you can only see a lunar eclipse at night. Unlike a solar eclipse, which may last only a few minutes, a lunar eclipse can last for up to 4 hours.

Most of Arybatha's ideas about astronomy are included in the two books written by Brahmagupta. The first, *The Opening of the Universe*, was completed in 628. His second text was finished in 665—just 5 years before he died. Surprisingly, Brahmagupta did not believe that Earth spins.

Although Johannes Kepler was the first European to suggest that planets orbit in ellipses rather than circles, this idea had been suggested in *Arybhatiya* 1,000 years earlier.

A Look at the Planets

In his book, Brahmagupta described the positions and movements of Mercury, Venus, Mars, and Jupiter. (The other planets were not discovered until after the telescope was invented in the 1600s.) While Arybhata's book does not describe planetary movements in great detail, it suggests that the planets' orbits are shaped like *ellipses,* rather than circles. It is truely amazing that this idea occurred to someone living 1,500 years ago. Johannes Kepler, who lived about 500 years ago, was the first European astronomer to come to this conclusion.

People have always been curious about the size and shape of our planet. Careful observers living in the earliest civilizations thought the world was round. When they looked at Earth's shadow on the moon during an eclipse, they saw that it was curved. Only a sphere could create that type of shadow. Other observers noticed that as a ship approached the shore, its tall sails came into view before the ship's hull. This suggested that the ship was sailing on a curved sea. Despite this evidence, up to the 1400s, many people believed the world was flat.

Brahmagupta knew that the world was round. Using a combination of mathematical and astronomical knowledge, he estimated that Earth's circumference was about 5,000 yojanas. If one yojana equals about 4.5 miles (7.2 km), what was Brahmagupta's estimate for the distance around Earth? Today, we know that Earth's circumference is about 24,860 miles (40,000 km). How close was Brahmagupta?

Developing a Calendar

Calendars were as important to the ancient Indians as they are to us today. They helped farmers decide when to plant crops. Travelers and traders used calendars to determine when they could safely cross snow-covered mountains and blazing deserts. And everyone used them to know when important festivals would take place.

For centuries, the Indians used the phases of the moon to measure the passage of time. They divided each 30-day month into two 15-day periods. The Indian year, which was 12 months long, was divided into six seasons. Each season was 2 months long.

A year consisting of 12 months that are 30 days long is 360 days long. However, the calendar we use today is 365 days long. This 5-day difference may not seem like such a big deal, but take a minute to think what that would mean. If every year were 5 days shorter, there would come a time when May would fall in the middle of winter and November would be during late summer.

Clearly, such a calendar could not be used to predict when the weather would be right for sowing seeds or harvesting crops. To fix this problem, the Indians added an extra month to their calendar every 30 months. This "leap" month made the calendar year almost exactly equal to the amount of time it takes Earth to circle the sun.

Although the ancient Indians had a fairly accurate calendar thousands of years ago, Arybhata was the first to calculate the length of a year. In *Arybhatiya,* he recorded the length of a year as 365 days, 6 hours, 12 minutes, and 30 seconds. Later Brahmagupta came up with a slightly different estimate. He believed the year was 365 days, 6 hours, 5 minutes, and 19 seconds long. Today we know that the true length of a solar year is a little less than 365 days and 6 hours.

Arybhata and Brahmagupta contributed a great deal to Indian mathematics and astronomy, but their contributions did not end there. As you will learn in the next chapter, Brahmagupta also studied the physical forces that affect objects on Earth and throughout the universe.

chapter 5
Understanding the Physical World

Brahmagupta believed that objects fall to
Earth for the same reason that water flows,
because that is the natural state of things.

than a shoe box full of rocks, even though the boxes are the same size. This idea also explains why very hot food is more likely to melt a plastic fork than a metal fork.

Kanada was not the only ancient philosopher to suggest that all matter is made up of atoms. A Greek philosopher named Democritus also wrote about this idea. It is impossible to say whether the idea was carried from India to Greece or whether each man came up with the idea on his own. As you learned earlier, after Alexander the Great invaded northern India, the Greeks became increasingly interested in trading with the Indians. We know they prized Indian perfumes, spices, and fabrics, but just how many philosophical ideas passed from one culture to the other is unknown.

A bust of Democritus

chapter 6
What India Gave the World

An Indian man sitting in a yoga
position with his feet behind his
head

It is clear that ancient India made many important contributions to modern science. The counting system we use every day comes from India, as does algebra. The origins of yoga as well as some of our modern medications and surgical techniques can also be traced to ancient India.

Other scientific discoveries seem to have developed first in India, but did not reach Europe for thousands of years. Indian stargazers were among the first to understand Earth's position in the universe and to know what causes an eclipse. They also knew the length of a year and the circumference of Earth. The ancient Indians even understood gravity. By the time this knowledge reached Europe, it had been discovered independently by scientists in other parts of the world.

The origins of still other ideas, such as the proper treatment of patients and the existence of atoms, remain unclear. These ideas may have traveled from India to Greece—or from Greece and India—more than 2,500 years ago. It is important to realize that many major scientific findings may have had more than one place of origin. In some cases, great thinkers in different parts of the world made a discovery at about the same time. In other cases, a person in one part of the world developed a new idea after reading a document written by someone in another part of the world. Like spices, gems, and precious metals, scientific ideas were often carried from one ancient civilization to another by travelers and traders.

The Price of Foreign Rule

Clearly, the scientific knowledge of the ancient Indians was once far superior to that of the Europeans. So why isn't that true today? In the 1500s,

This painting, completed in 1510 by the Italian artist Raphael, shows the great scholars of ancient Greece.

European science began to advance more rapidly than Indian science. As Europe entered a period called the Renaissance, philosophers and scientists began to study the vast knowledge accumulated hundreds of years earlier by the ancient Greeks and Romans.

At the same time, Europeans began to discover and conquer other areas of the world. They borrowed the scientific ideas that had been developed by people living in the Americas, the Middle East, China, and India.

Although the Indians continued to study and make discoveries about the world around them, the Muslim and European rulers that controlled most of India between 711 and 1947 were not interested in supporting scientific studies.

Emperor Shah Jahan, a Muslim, was the leader of the Mughal Empire in the early 1600s. The Mughal Empire controlled most of India from 1526 to 1707.

An official of the British East India Company riding on an elephant

The East India Company, established by the British in 1600, invested most of its resources in developing agriculture in India. When India became a British colony in 1858, little changed. Only recently has Indian science begun to flourish again.

GLOSSARY

algebra—a form of arithmetic in which letters represent numbers.

Arabic numerals—the system of numbers that we use in modern mathematics. It was developed in ancient India and brought to Europe by the Muslims, who were also called Arabs.

archaeologist—a scientist who studies past human life and activities.

area—the amount of space enclosed by a shape.

astronomer—a scientist who studies stars and planets.

atom—the smallest unit of an element that still has all the properties of the element.

ayurveda—the system of medicine practiced by the ancient Indians. The literal meaning of the word is "the science of long life."

bile—a yellow or greenish fluid produced by the liver and used during digestion.

caste—one of the social groupings into which many Indians are divided. The caste system has its origins in the *Vedas*, which recognized four castes. Today there are hundreds of castes in India. Most are determined by a person's occupation. Even though all Indians are not members of a specific caste, all are affected by the caste system. This is the major reason why the Hindu way of life continues to have tremendous influence over everyone in India, regardless of their religious beliefs.

cataract—a clouding of the lens of the eye that prevents light from passing through and impairs vision.

circumference—the distance around the widest part of Earth or any other circular or spherical object.

civilization—a community of people with a relatively high level of cultural development.

ellipse—an oval drawn around two points.

epilepsy—a disease of the central nervous system. People with this condition experience periodic seizures.

erosion—the process by which water washes away dirt and rock.

genetics—the study of how characteristics are passed from parent to child.

gravitational field—the area over which an object's gravitational force can influence other objects.

gravity—the force of attraction between objects.

jaundice—a disease characterized by yellowish-colored skin, tissues, and body fluids. It occurs when the liver produces too much bile and some of this fluid leaks into various parts of the body.

karma—according to Hinduism and Buddhism, the force generated by a person's actions that determines what the person's life will be like when he or she is reincarnated.

leprosy—an infectious disease that primarily affects the skin.

lunar eclipse—when the moon is hidden by a shadow cast by Earth as it moves between the sun and the moon.

Muslim—a person who follows the faith of Islam.

nirvana—the final goal of Hindus and Buddhists; the end of the reincarnation cycle.

philosopher—a person who studies reality and the nature of truth.

place value—the value given to a digit as a result of its position in a number. In 71, the place value of 7 is tens. In 718, the place value of 7 is hundreds.

reincarnation—according to Hinduism and Buddhism, when a person's soul is reborn one or more times in various bodies.

solar eclipse—when the moon moves between Earth and the sun.

volume—the amount of space occupied by an object.

RESOURCES

Books

Beshore, George. *Science in Early Islamic Cultures*. Danbury, CT: Franklin Watts, 1998.

Carter, Ron. *Early Civilizations*. Morristown, NJ: Silver Burdett, 1980.

Colblence, Jean-Michel. *The Earliest Cities*. Morristown, NJ: Silver Burdett, 1987.

Ganeri, Anita. *Exploration into India*. New York: New Discovery Books, 1994.

Haskins, Jim. *Count Your Way Through India*. Minneapolis: Carolrhoda Books, Inc., 1990.

McNair, Sylvia. *India*. Chicago: Children's Press, 1990.

Internet Sites

Ancient India provides a 3,000-year timeline of major events in India as well as brief descriptions of Ancient Indian culture, sports, and religion. This site can be reached at **http://www.crystalinks.com/east.html**.

Exploring Ancient World Culure includes maps, timelines, essays, and images that describe ancient civilizations in India, China, Greece, and the Middle East. Its address is: **http://eawc.evansville.edu/index.htm**.

This site has all the text of a book called *India's Contribution to World Culture*, which was written by Sudheer Birodkar. The book describes India's contribution to mathematics, astronomy, medicine, chemistry, physics, engineering, philosophy, and more. It includes original text from Indian texts written more than 2,000 years ago. It can be reached at: **http://India.CoolAtlanta.com/Great Pages/sudheer/**.

This site has the text of an article called "Plastic Surgery's Earliest Cases Date to Ancient Egypt, India." The article appeared in *The Washington Post* on December 13, 1994. The address is: **http://rbhatnagar.ececs.uc.edu:8080/alt_hindu/1994_2/msg00097.html.**

INDEX

ABOUT THE AUTHOR

Melissa Stewart earned a Bachelor's degree in biology from Union College and a Master's degree in science and environmental journalism from New York University. She has been writing about science and health on a freelance basis for almost a decade. This is her second book for Franklin Watts.